COMBAT IN OUTNUMBERED SCENARIOS:

The origin of Historical Fencing

From traditional double handed weapons (staff)
To current single handed weapons (baton)

COMBAT IN OUTNUMBERED SCENARIOS:
The origin of Historical Fencing

From traditional double handed weapons (staff)
To current single handed weapons (baton)

by

Luís Franco Preto
MSc in Sports Training Sciences

Luís Franco Preto (1978 -)

To Master Nuno Curvello Russo

A brilliant martial artist and fierce fighter whose skills and knowledge will probably, like so many before him in all walks of life, only be fully appreciated once he's gone.

Master Nuno Curvello Russo
sparring against two opponents

Acknowledgments

I'd like to extend a heartfelt thanks to the following people for their help in gathering the photos for this book:

- Andy Fosmark

- Frederico Martins

- Julia Dordel

- (Master) Nuno Mota

- Roland Cooper

- Devon Boorman who, not only made himself available for the shoot, but also generously allowed the use of his Academie Duello's amazing facilities.

Table of contents

"There's a difference between interest and commitment.

When you're interested in doing something, you do it only when circumstance permit.

When you're committed to something, you accept no excuses, only results."

Art Turock

"Does history record any case in which the majority was right?"

Robert Heinlein

Introduction

The publishing of a book on Jogo do Pau and "its" system for outnumbered combat is equivalent to considering that it is a book on European Historical Fencing's origin. Cutting straight to the point, I state this because I consider that Jogo do Pau is Historical Fencing and Historical Fencing is Jogo do Pau, and here's why:

1) There are Portuguese documents which allow us to conclude that, as long sword medieval fencing systems were replaced within the military by firearms, they were kept alive by civilians through the use of staffs[1]. I myself am also capable of performing the exact same skills with both weapons.

- **Thus, the first conclusion that can be summarized from this is that:**

     Categorizing Jogo do Pau as "Portuguese staff exclusive fencing system" is incorrect.
     Jogo do Pau is actually a medieval fencing skill set which was historically applied to both long swords and staffs, depending on the social conditioning factors that determined which weapons were available.

2) Secondly, before the recent focus by the French on developing the combat sport Canne de Combat, France also used to have their own "staff fencing" art, with exactly the same name as the "Portuguese" Jogo do Pau, only in French, obviously! It was Le Jeux du Baton.

     It so happens that Nuno Curvello Russo, who is regarded as most experienced and knowledgeable Jogo do Pau instructor in Portugal, lived in France during the seventies and, while there, met Maurice Sarry. Like Russo, Sarry had dedicated himself to the extensive study of his country's traditional fighting art, being highly

---

[1] Strikes with these weapons share the same terminology as well as striking angles.

regarded on a national level. As these two great Masters got acquainted with one another, they decided to train together. Shortly after, they realized that all the traditional single combat techniques[2] that made up these two arts were absolutely identical.

Note that I specifically pointed out that I am referring to single combat technique because, at the time, the French art had become exclusively focused on this type of combat, similarly to what also occurred within Portugal's urban industrial cities[3].

- **Hence, the second conclusion that can be summarized from this is that:**

Jogo do Pau is a European Fencing Art, and not merely a Portuguese one. Consequently, this means that European Fencing is Jogo do Pau.

Please note that I do not wish to sound, even if for just for a second, disrespectful towards other European systems, such as the German and Italian. Though they are also European Historical Fencing, I consider that, just like that which occurs amongst other motor activities, there is one common set of technical foundations that can be used under different tactical perspectives, which is the element responsible for bringing about distinct styles[4]. Thus, Jogo do Pau's "style" of performing European Historical Fencing gathers a set of guiding principles pertaining universal concepts such as distance, timing, parrying and striking angles – to name just a few – that characterize both its specific practice as well as European Historical Fencing as a whole.

Furthermore, I consider that this specific topic of outnumbered combat represents the origin of Historical Fencing given that:

1) As a whole, mankind began its martial exploits by focusing on developing combat skill against multiple opponents.

From its first days, mankind has always had the need to, not only hunt, but also fight other human beings so as to either protect or conquer both assets and territory. Hence, military conflicts which took place during medieval times were focused around

---

[2] Strikes, parries & footwork.
[3] Where the practice of Jogo do Pau for "mere" leisure resulted in the sole practice of single combat.
[4] Instead of distinct arts altogether.

battlefield combat, meaning that people had to be ready to fight many opponents approaching simultaneously from many different directions. Consequently, martial arts' origin and essence resides in the development of effective combat skills that allow one to successfully overcome such scenarios.

Plus, even within civilian environments, the most common self defence setting entails having to defend oneself against a higher number of opponents who wish to steal the outnumbered combatant's assets.

Given this, it makes perfect sense to assume that the development of combat skill within European fencing arts was, similarly to "Portugal's" Jogo do Pau, initially geared towards the study of technical and tactical skills that best fit the success and constraining variables that characterize outnumbered combat.

At the same time, outnumbered combat also corresponds to one of my favourite topics within martial arts. In absolute honesty, having practiced Asian martial arts under circumstances that only had me dealing with imaginary opponents, having to manage real opponents was one of the main things that attracted me to Jogo do Pau. In this regard, I find that this is a topic commonly lacking a good enough understanding by a large portion of the martial arts' world and, therefore, in desperate need of clarification. Hence, it is with an enormous passion and feeling of relevance towards this topic that I will present Jogo do Pau's[5] concepts on outnumbered combat.

Understanding the history behind the art's skill development

Before actually analysing the variables behind this topic's motor skills, one historical element need to be clarified about Jogo do Pau.

This art was born and developed way before the industrial revolution took place, meaning that most people still lived in rural environments where they:

1) Carried long walking staffs that, in the absence of swords, were extremely useful for combat,

---

[5] Historical Fencing's

2) Usually, had no shortage of space to swing such weapons, which explains the system's strong reliance on wide striking motions.

Consequently, having the present analysis of outnumbered combat highlighting the art's history by being initially focused on long double handed weapons should come as no surprise.

However, given that Portugal also underwent the industrial revolution, the recent development of cities where people replaced the traditional walking staffs with walking canes brought about the application of the art's "traditional" double handed weapons' contents to these shorter one handed weapons[6]. Therefore, over the course of this book, I shall also cover the contents pertaining to single handed weapons' outnumbered combat skill set which, despite resembling that of the staff, has some particularities which need specific analysis and training.

In the last section I shall explain how outnumbered and single combat are historically and technically connected. Such analysis will include a reflexion on how the development of outnumbered combat's combat skills influenced the development of combat skill for single combat.

It is my hope that you enjoy reading this book and that it may influence your martial training by making it even more interesting and fun.

---

[6] With most of the research within this field having been performed by Master Nuno Curvello Russo, still alive and regarded as the most skilled and knowledgeable instructor to date.

Self defence oriented philosophy

I find that, for people to really understand martial arts from a combat perspective, it is useful to compare it with trapeze artists.

Over time, one detail has changed regarding the conditions under which these artists perform, which has been the introduction of safety nets. The introduction of this piece of equipment makes its practice much safer and, consequently, reduces the psychological stress levels experienced before each performance[7].

Personally, I look at martial artists' preparation for self defence combat as the development of the ability to fight without a safety net, independently of facing one or ten opponents[8]. Sometimes, one opponent can even turn out to be more dangerous than ten, not only due to his / her skill level, but also due to the impossibility of guessing whether the lone opponent has either a hidden weapon or nearby friends ready to help out.

Additionally, no matter how many times one happens to be fed contemporary martial arts' all too common misconceptions of unbeatable systems and foolproof techniques, such myths usually have little, if any, similarity with the cruel and ugly reality of actual violence.

Therefore, outnumbered combat's first guideline consists of the following premise:

The only foolproof strategy that will guaranty one's safety is to avoid being involved in physical conflicts altogether. Consequently, people should mainly try to avoid conflicts and, whenever that fails, they should, first and foremost, look to escape[9].

---

[7] By heavily reducing the risk of sustaining terrible injuries or even death.

[8] Just like with trapeze artists, one only has to miss once for it to be game over but, in this case, with combatants' being on the line.

[9] Self defence conflicts are not a competition of egos or, at least, they shouldn't be.

For several different reasons, one may occasionally be left with no other option but to fight and, whenever that occurs, it is crucial that people fight to win by not holding anything back! Nevertheless, I have known a few individuals who deliberately look to fight so as to feed their ego, which results in having them unnecessarily adding more wood to a fire[10] that could, and should, be put out using simpler and safer strategies. Ultimately, these people end up fighting more often than needed and, consequently, many end up either dead or in prison, meaning that:

Avoidance and running away whenever possible is just a matter of being smart, not weak[11]!

Ultimately, this philosophical discussion ends up boiling down to the well known choice between "living to fight or fighting to live". However, as already mentioned, there will always be some situations in which fighting is unavoidable and, very often, while having to face a higher number of opponents. Thus, let us proceed with the analysis of the specific techniques and strategies that offer combatants the best chance[12] of overcoming such challenges.

---

[10] Conflict.

[11] Plus, considering that, as previously stated, some individuals force conflicts due to self esteem issues, admitting such problems can actually require greater strength than that which is needed to fuel one hundred physical conflicts.

[12] Though not full.

Theoretical principals

Fighting one opponent of the same skill level is a dangerous scenario in which combatants have, at best, a fifty percent chance of success. Thus, when facing multiple opponents, the outnumbered combatant's chances decrease with every new opponent that is added. This obviously reinforces the previously mentioned self defence philosophy of privileging avoidance and escape strategies. Nevertheless, it may happen that the way to do so is being blocked by the group of opponents. Should that occur, how should outnumbered combatants engage and manage their opponents while still looking for a way to escape?

Are opponents standing at a distance of five meters considered an immediate threat[13]? Baring the use of projectiles[14], such opponents will have to start by getting closer in order to perform both grappling and striking techniques with either their limbs or striking weapons at their specific reach.

**Combatants positioned at a distance
higher than their reach**

A)

---

[13] In the sense of expecting that person to be capable of performing a strike from where he / she is.
[14] Stones, arrows, bullets or any ordinary object laying around.

B)

This means that whenever combatants are able to keep their opponents at a distance they will, at least, avoid getting hit. Consequently:

> ***Outnumbered combatants' strategy needs to consist of keeping opponents at a distance while looking for an opening to escape.***

While doing so, should the opponents make mistakes that place them in unfavourable situations, outnumbered combatants should try to capitalize by striking them. However, it is crucial to look at such scenarios as bonuses that take place due to opponents' mistakes. Otherwise, should combatants approach outnumbered combat expecting to be capable of striking their foes, they will end up forcing unfavourable offensive situations[15] which will end up placing them in danger.

Assuming that, up until this point, everything has been pretty much straight forward, we are now left with understanding how this strategy is put into practice. Though it is not rocket science, it does require some studying and practice. Therefore, let us pull up our sleeves and get down right to it.

---

[15] Which include failing to take advantage of clear opportunities to escape that come about while sparring.

Putting theory into practice

Engaging multiple opponents

Awareness

Every martial system is based on certain principles to be effective. Although these principles may vary somewhat between systems, there is one principle which I consider universal, and that is awareness.

Unfortunately, it is very common for people within the martial arts community to showcase greater concern with learning how to solve impossible or near impossible scenarios than with learning how to prevent them. How many times have you heard a martial arts' student asking about the miraculous technique for when being controlled from behind and, quite often, while being chocked by someone double his / her size and strength? Real fighting is much tougher than the image created by martial arts' movies and later perpetuated by numerous instructors. Therefore:

> ## _People ought to, first and foremost, look to prevent and avoid conflicts_!

If one neglects awareness and avoidance and, as such, trains by assuming that he / she will forcefully end up in these dreadful situations, then it is very likely that such scenarios do end up materializing. However, when confronted with real violence, most people end up going through a very hard reality check which has them realizing that overcoming the odds against a non compliant opponent as easy as in practice.

Thus, the first and universal principal on which all martial systems should be based is awareness. It shouldn't be expected to consistently win fights by always having to beat the odds, much less survive for very long, if one consistently let him or herself to be surprised from behind, hit on the head with a beer bottle and kicked by three hooligans at the same time! Hence, in order to have a good chance of successfully overcoming multiple opponents, combatants must start by detecting them, and preferably at a distance. Otherwise, it will simply be an old fashion ambush and, unless one happens to be dealing with complete amateurs and idiots[16], the outcome will not be at all favourable.

Nevertheless, although awareness can and SHOULD be trained, its training methodology is something that I find to be outside the scope of this book and, therefore, I will assume that trainees are already able to practice and perform this skill, which leads us directly to the art's actual combat contents.

Engagement through distance management

Phase one

With a partner, place yourselves at some five to ten meters away from each other. Then, with one being the attacker, he / she will have the task of approaching and delivering a strike. This should play out by having the attacker taking several approaching steps while holding his / her weapon in a forward pointing waiting guard position. As the weapons' forward tips are about to touch, the attacker should perform one final approaching step while also striking.

During this first practice phase, the defender should remain on the same spot so that the attacker is able to land a controlled strike and, therefore, receive visual feedback at the end of the strike regarding the technique's spatial management[17].

---

[16] Which is rarely the case, given that such subjects have, usually, already been eliminated by "natural selection".

[17] In terms of distance and placement.

**Being out of striking distance,
the "attacker" starts by approaching before striking
(Double handed weapons)**

A)

B)

C)

D)

E)

F)

Being out of striking distance,
the "attacker" starts by approaching before striking
(Single handed weapons)

A)

B)

C)

D)

E)

F)

Phase two

Afterwards, repeat the same exercise but, as the attacker is approaching, the defender[18] will look to detect when the attacker starts performing the last approaching step in a waiting guard stance[19]. As the attacker starts that stepping motion, the defender should release a strike of his /her own while also stepping forward.

By performing this type of pre-emptive striking motion, combatants are able to use distance together with their opponent's approach in their favour so as to pre-emptively release a strike that takes the approaching attacker completely by surprise. The combatant reacting to the opponent's approach is also able to force a change of roles by relegating the "attacker" to a defensive and REACTIVE role.

Thus, when facing multiple opponents, and assuming that the lone combatant was able to detect the opponents at a distance, this is how to engage them. Nevertheless, let us analyze this topic in more detail.

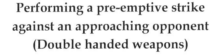

**Performing a pre-emptive strike
against an approaching opponent
(Double handed weapons)**

A)

---

[18] Who used his / her "passive" role during the previous phase in order to become visually familiarized with the attacker's approach.

[19] Overall, the second to last approaching step, before the final approaching step which is performed while already attacking.

B)

C)

D)

Performing a pre-emptive strike against an approaching opponent
(Single handed weapons)

A)

B)

C)

D)

E)

Understanding this tactic's premises

By staying put, distant from the opponents, one transmits the message:

"If you guys want me, come and get me".

This way, by either standing still or even stepping back[20], combatants not only force their opponents to approach, but they even induce them to base their approaching on slightly incorrect premises. This initial data induces attackers to consider that their target is, not only out of striking reach, but also not approaching. Consequently, they will fall into the trap of thinking that they will have to carry out the shortening of combat distance by themselves in order to place the lone combatant within striking reach. Hence, due to this false assumption, the outnumbered combatant is able to turn these conditions to his / her advantage by performing a pre-emptive strike that places his / her opponents in a defensive and reactive role.

This is the main guiding principle that combatants should look to perform when engaging multiple opponents. However, before putting it to practice, trainees need to become acquainted with the main technique which is to be performed both afterwards and, sometimes, during the actual initial engagement phase.

Luring in opponents so as to force them into a defensive and reactive role

A)

---

[20] So as to be positioned even further away from the opponents' striking distance.

B)

C)

D)

E)

Outnumbered combat's techniques – section one

Sweep from above

Staff

In pairs, one student positions his / her weapon forward and upward so as to simulate an incoming strike. The other starts by placing his / her dominant leg forward and the weapon pointing backwards, while slightly above his / her head on his / her non dominant side.

Standard initial stance

From this position, trainees should extend their upper limbs forward so as to use both weapons to visually verify their distance towards their partner[21].

---

[21] Which should consist of having the weapons' forward extremities touching.

**Measuring the initial distance
from which to start this exercise**

After adjusting distance, trainees should return to the previously described overhead backward pointing waiting guard in order to practice the sweep from above.

The sweep from above consists a first half rotational oblique descending strike, meant to sweep the opponent's weapon from in front of you, followed by a second, and this time, full rotational strike towards the opponent's body.

Therefore, the initial half rotational strike is to be performed without stepping forward[22], since one's goal is to simply intercept the opponent's weapon and such task can already be successfully performed from the position one is starting from.

First phase of the sweep from above

A)

B)

---

[22] Merely moving the centre of gravity slightly forward.

C)

Then, upon finishing this motion, one's weapon does not stop and, by pulling the upper limbs back and releasing them forward again, trainees follow through with a full rotational strike on the same side. However, this time the technique is to target the opponent's body, which will warrant a full approaching step.

After an initial introduction to this exercise where the training partner serving as target does not exit[23], continue performing the drill but with the person serving as a target stepping out of striking distance to start with and, later, parrying him / herself from the strike while exiting [24].

---

[23] So that trainees manage to perform the sweep from above while being given an objective visual feedback as to its spatial management (distancing and placement).
[24] Given that, in live sparring at maximum speed, the exiting may occasionally be a bit late and, should that be the case, it needs to be complemented with a parry.

Second phase of the sweep from above, directing the strike towards the opponent's head or knee

A)

B)

C1)

C2)

**Performing the sweep from above
with the opponent exiting so as to avoid being hit**

A)

B)

C)

D)

E)

F)

G)

Baton

Sweep from above on non dominant side

Performing the sweep from above with the baton follows the main overall concept previously presented for the staff, requiring only two slight adjustments.

Standard initial stance with the baton

Since this is a one handed weapon, performers will be unable to stop their upper limb's motion in a forward extended position as the initial half rotational strike[25] intercepts the opponent's weapon. Consequently, combatants should allow for the baton to naturally swing upwards as their flex their upper limb in order to, once again, powerfully release their weapon forward.

---

[25] Given that the motion's kinetic energy will force it to continue towards the dominant side and, in the present case, also downwards.

Sweep from above on the non dominant side
with single handed weapons

A)

B)

C)

D)

E)

Sweep from above on dominant side

Afterwards, it is also necessary to train the same technique on the opposite side, which is obviously done by placing the non dominant lower limb forward and the baton, once again, pointing backwards, only on the dominant side.

Thus, this time around, the half rotational sweep is released on the dominant side and the counter attack on the non dominant, with both strikes' trajectories being oblique descending ones.

**Sweep from above on the dominant side
with single handed weapons**

A)

B)

C)

D)

E)

F)

Application of the sweep from above against two opponents

<u>*Phase one*</u>

Now, in groups of three, the outnumbered combatant should be in the middle, with one opponent in front and the other one behind.

**Starting position in order to apply
the sweep from above against two opponents**

Facing one of the opponents, the outnumbered combatant should perform the sweep from above, thus sweeping the opponent's weapon with the first motion and finishing the approaching step with the counter attack[26].

---

[26] Which the opponent avoids by stepping back and, eventually, also parrying.

Sweep from above against the opponent on the right

A)

B)

C)

D)

E)

As depicted in the previous photos, the performance of the sweep from above allows for the outnumbered combatant to push one opponent away while, simultaneously, stepping out of the other opponent's striking distance. As the second strike lands, the outnumbered combatant should rotate his / her neck towards his / her dominant side, so as to observe the opponent approaching from behind.

Finishing the sweep from above while looking:
At the opponent being attacked (A)
Towards the one approaching from behind (B)

A)

B)

As the opponent is approaching from behind, the outnumbered combatant must transfer his / her centre of gravity towards his / her dominant leg, so as to follow through with yet another sweep from above[27].

---

[27] With the full rotational strike being, once again, performed during the forward step.

Using the increased distance towards the opponent approaching from behind in order to pre-emptively strike him / her

A)

B)

C)

D)

E)

F)

This will enable for the outnumbered combatant to push away the approaching opponent, at the same time that he / she is, once again, able to step out of the other opponent's striking distance.

By continuously performing sweeps from above both opponents are kept at bay. However, as everyone easily comes to realize, this ends up being significantly more tiring for the outnumbered combatant, which is why we need to, once again, reinforce that:

__Upon gaining enough space and time to escape, outnumbered combatants should immediately do so.__

Lining up opponents

One final note is probably in order concerning the well known strategy of lining up opponents.

I believe that some readers might be already criticizing the previously described engagement strategy, given that it implies having the outnumbered combatant placing him / herself between his / her opponents, instead of having trying to line them up so as to fight one at a time.

It so happens that combatants who are truly motivated to really hurt their outnumbered opponent and, once again, aren't complete idiots, will look to surround they "prey". Therefore, even if one does try to line them up, they will react by adjusting their positioning as well, instead of passively just allowing themselves to be lined up. This analysis and experience of how fighting really does develop brought about the decision of channelling our tactical reasoning in order to develop the ability to handle the circumstance of being surrounded from the very beginning.

Lining up two passive opponents

A)

B)

C)

D)

Lining up two non passive opponents

A)

B)

C)

D)

Phase two

In combat, like in most competitive sports, speed is fundamental. Fencing arts are no different and, when combatants are forced to fight multiple opponents simultaneously, it becomes even more important.

Therefore, in order to successfully manage multiple opponents, it is necessary to improve the performance of the sweep from above by going from looking at the opponent located at the backside after finishing the sweep from above, to finishing the second strike of the sweep from above while already looking at the opponent approaching from behind. For most people, this is especially difficult to perform due to emotional constraining factors. For the most part, finishing striking techniques while looking in the opposite direction makes people quite uncomfortable, given that most are worried about not injuring their training partners and, by looking somewhere else when landing strikes, they are unable to do so if needed.

However, such a concern shows a training attitude which is, not only the opposite of what should be combatants' frame of mind[28], but also one that induces the development of an incorrect technique. Obviously, I agree that, given these activities' special nature, training will not last if some control is not exerted on most occasions. Nevertheless, trainees are better off using simple exercises such as this one to assume that everything will turn out ok [29]and, consequently, perform their strikes correctly by means of having them going through their opponent as they are already looking the other way.

If, nevertheless, some concerns do still exist in the beginning, it is preferable to start training slowly but correctly and, as confidence grows regarding one's partners' ability to exit, increase execution speed.

---

[28] Looking to control strikes instead of actively striving to the best of their ability to actually land them successfully.
[29] Given that they are dealing with very simple tactical behaviours.

Improving technique by going from finishing the first strike looking ahead (B) to being already observing the opponent(s) approaching from behind (C)

A)

B)

C)

Practical settings of engaging multiple opponents

After analysing and discussing the main principle of engaging opponents by means of using distance management to optimize the performance of pre-emptive strikes, let us see how to actually perform this principle against multiple opponents.

Staff

Having one's opponents positioning themselves away from each other[30], the outnumbered combatant should react by positioning him / herself in a forward pointing waiting guard while in a non dominant lower limb lead stance. Additionally, the outnumbered combatant also needs to ensure that he / she is facing the middle, instead of facing one of the opponents. Doing so allows for outnumbered combatants to observe both approaching opponents simultaneously.

Correct (A) & incorrect (B) positioning in order to control the approach of both opponents

A)

---

[30] Under the goal of surrounding their prey.

B)

When fighting with staffs, combatants should:

1) Control the opponents' approach in order to detect which one is the quickest to get closer,

2) Upon diagnosing which one is closest, perform a strike against this opponent.

The development of this skill within a controlled and systematized training environment should entail the practice of the following two scenarios.

Scenario A

    a) As an introductory drill, have the opponent on your non dominant side[31] approach.

    As he / she does so, start by performing an oblique descending strike on the dominant side, together with a double half step in this opponent's direction. By performing this step, instead of a passing step, outnumbered combatants are able to finish their initial strike without having their back turned to the other opponent.

---

[31] The side opposite to that of your weapon.

Then, in order to have a wider approaching reach[32], progress by adjusting this approaching double half step in the following manner:

- Have the back leg initially move behind the lead leg in the opponent's direction,

- Follow this initial step by moving the lead leg in the same direction, just as previously practiced,

- Finally, as you perform this adapted double stepping action, add a third side step with the back leg, again, cross stepping behind the lead leg.

Performing this final step allows for combatants to position themselves at a better angle so as to have a higher chance of keeping all opponents in their field of view[33].

Opponent on the right approaches

A)

---

[32] In order to be capable of taking the initiative with the opponents further away.
[33] Especially those approaching on the dominant side and, eventually, also from behind. This latter circumstance will start occurring more often when, later on, trainees start training against more than two opponents.

B)

**Incorrectly striking by taking a single step,
which makes it harder to control and move towards the other opponent**

A)

B)

C)

D)

E)

Approaching the opponent on the right
by taking a double half step

A)

B)

C)

D)

Taking the initiative by moving the back leg
behind the lead leg for a higher stride length

A)

B)

C)

Three step engaging motion
for better positioning

A)

B)

C)

D)

Scenario B

This time around, it should be the other opponent, who is standing on the outnumbered combatant's dominant side, to approach first.

**Opponent on the left
being the first to approach**

A)

B)

In this case, the outnumbered combatant should simply lift his / her weapon so as to have it pointing backwards on the non dominant side and, from this position, perform a sweep from above. However, due to the wider distance between the outnumbered combatants and his / her opponents, the sweep from above will require the performance of two full approaching steps, one with each strike.

Performing the sweep from above in other to push the opponent on the left away, while also increasing the distance towards the opponent on the right

A)

B)

C)

D)

E)

F)

G)

H)

After clearly performing this first sweep from above in the "attacker's" direction, so as to push him / her away at the same time that the distance towards the other opponent is increased, the outnumbered combatant should immediately perform another sweep from above towards the other opponent, the one approaching from behind. Doing so allows for the outnumbered combatant to spread the opponents a bit more and, therefore, generate more space which, in turn, increases the time available to manage them.

Nevertheless, as the outnumbered combatant finishes the first sweep from above, he / she needs to move the back leg so as to immediately square off with the other opponent and, thus, manage to quickly follow through with another a sweep from above.

In order to get a better grip on these contents, trainees should practice them by alternating between taking the initiative against both opponents, given that doing so makes it easier for trainees to memorize these new skills.

Afterward doing so during an introductory phase trainees should have their opponents randomly approaching, since that will force the outnumbered combatant to develop the ability to read which opponent is approaching first.

**Pushing the opponent on the right away,
while stepping out of the other opponent's reach**

A)

B)

C)

D)

E)

Baton

Though taking the initiative with the baton against multiple opponents follows the same principles, it still requires a few adjustments.

Adjusting footwork

When fighting with batons, instead of always moving the back leg to start with, outnumbered combatants should start by moving the leg which is closest to the opponent one is approaching. Quite naturally, this entails stepping with the left leg when moving to the left side and, alternatively, stepping with the right leg when moving to the right side.

Hence, when moving towards the lead leg's side, outnumbered combatants will be merely sliding the lead leg in the "attacker's" direction. Therefore, outnumbered combatants will have less reach on this side than when taking the initiative against the opponent on the back leg's side[34]. Consequently, outnumbered combatants need to factor in this additional variable, instead of merely diagnosing which opponent is closer. Ultimately, this means that, with the baton, outnumbered combatants will end up favouring their back leg's side and, consequently, resort to taking the initiative towards the opponent on their lead leg's side only when that opponent is significantly closer than the remaining opponents.

Engaging the opponent on the right by sliding lead leg

A)

---

[34] On which outnumbered combatants take a full step forward with their back leg.

B)

C)

D)

Engaging the opponent on the left

A)

B)

C)

D)

Adjusting striking technique

Since the baton is shorter than the staff, combat distance will also be shorter and, consequently, sparring will also be faster. Therefore, it is highly likely that the group of assailants will be approaching by being closer together, which makes it extremely difficult to start off by performing a full double strike sweep from above. Hence, outnumbered combatants should perform the following alternative strategies:

1) Unleash merely one strike towards the first attacker that moves into striking reach[35] and, upon completing this strike, immediately follow through with:

    a) A full double sweep strike against the other opponent[36].

2) Perform a single strike towards both opponents, so as to push each of them a bit further away. This will obviously spread the opponents just enough to allow for the performance of a full double strike sweep from above, this time towards the opponent against whom the outnumbered combatant performed the initial strike.

These adjustments, characteristic of shorter one handed weapons, will force outnumbered combatants to be capable of performing the sweep from above on both sides[37].

---

[35] So as to push him / her away.

[36] Which manages to successfully spread the group of assailants and position the outnumbered combatant between his / her opponents.

[37] Given that, when the spatial conditions need so as to perform a full double strike sweep from above come along, outnumbered combatants' weapon will vary between being placed on the left and right sides.

Pushing one opponent away (the one on the right) before performing a full double strike technique

A)

B)

C)

D)

E)

F)

G)

H)

I)

**Pushing one opponent away (the one on the left)
before performing the double strike technique**

A)

B)

C)

D)

E)

F)

G)

H)

I)

**Performing just one strike against each opponent before committing
to the double strike sweep from above against the opponent initially attacked**

A)

B)

C)

D)

E)

F)

Outnumbered combat's techniques – section two

The backward sweep

Staff

**Initial stance for the performance
of the upcoming building steps**

Step one

From a non dominant leg lead stance, perform an oblique descending strike on the dominant side.

Step two

From the same non dominant lead leg stance, take a step back with the lead leg.

Step three

Afterwards, perform the same back stepping technique only, this time, finishing the back step facing backwards.

Step one – Oblique descending strike on the dominant side

A)

B)

C)

Step two – Full backwards step

A)

B)

C)

Step three – Finishing the back step facing backwards

A)

B)

C)

Step four

Merge the striking technique initially practiced with the back step.

Step five

Bring everything together by performing the striking technique towards the backside.

Step four – Merging the striking technique with the backstep

A)

B)

C)

Step five – Performing the striking technique towards the backside

A)

B)

C)

Baton

Once again, fighting with the baton requires a few adjustments, this time regarding the backward sweep, which brings about two ways of performing it.

<u>Option A</u>

When the second strike of the sweep from above is not blocked by the outnumbered combatant's opponents, both the weapon and the outnumbered combatant's upper limb will naturally follow through their motion from the side they started from to the opposite side and, given that the strike is an oblique descending one, also downwards.

**Performing the sweep from above
without having the second strike blocked**

A)

B)

C)

D)

Since the upper limb reaches the side opposite to the one where it started from before the weapon's forward tip, outnumbered combatants should raise their upper limb above the head as the weapon's forward tip moves past the opponent they are attacking. Doing so allows for outnumbered combatants to take advantage of the weapon's momentum so as to fluidly follow through with the performance of a backward sweep that has the weapon undergoing a full overhead rotation.

Following the sweep from above
with an overhead rotational backwards sweep

A)

B)

C)

D)

E)

Option B

Alternatively, outnumbered combatant's opponents are, occasionally, able to block the outnumbered combatant's second strike of the sweep from above. When this happens, outnumbered combatants are forced to perform a backward sweep that has the weapon moving directly from the previous strike's end position towards the opponent approaching from behind.

**Should the above sweep's second strike be blocked,
the backwards sweep is to be performed without any rotation**

A)

B)

C)

D)

E)

As was the case with the sweep from above, outnumbered combatants also need to practice the backward sweep with the baton on the opposite side[38].

---

[38] So that they are able to perform the wider range of options included within single handed weapons.

Backward sweep on the opposite side, after having the weapon blocked

A)

B)

C)

D)

E)

F)

G)

H)

I)

J)

K)

L)

Application of the backward sweep in combat against two opponents

Staff

With the outnumbered combatant positioned between two opponents, he / she should perform sequences of three sweeps: two sweeps from above[39] and one backward sweep, this one against the opponent against whom the outnumbered combatant performed the first sweep from above.

The tactical purpose of this sequence is to use the combination of the sweeps from above to push one of the attackers away while immediately getting out of his / her striking distance. Consequently, upon finishing the second sweep from above, the outnumbered combatant will have created enough space and time to surprise the opponent initially attacked with a strike opposite to that of the sweep from above.

After finishing the first sweep from above towards the opponent on the left, the outnumbered combatant should square of with the other opponent by reacquiring the same waiting guard

A)

---

[39] One against each opponent.

B)

C)

D)

E)

F)

After performing two sweeps from above, outnumbered combatants
should follow through with a backwards sweep

A)

B)

C)

D)

Baton

In order to start developing the understanding and skill of how to apply the backwards sweep when fighting with batons, repeat the drill described for the staff only with the opponents varying between blocking and merely avoiding[40] the outnumbered combatant's sweep from above. Doing so will teach trainees to read and distinguish between both situations and, consequently, follow through with each context specific variant of the backward sweep.

Phase 1

After pushing away the opponent on the right, the outnumbered combatant performs a sweep from above towards the opponent on the left

A)

B)

---

[40] By simply stepping out of distance.

C)

D)

E)

F)

G)

Phase 2 a)

After performing the second sweep from above, and having had the strike blocked, the outnumbered combatant is forced to perform a direct backward sweep

A)

B)

C)

D)

E)

F)

G)

H)

I)

Phase 2b)

After performing the second sweep from above and not having the weapon blocked, the outnumbered performs a rotational backward sweep

A)

B)

C)

D)

E)

F)

G)

H)

I)

Adding a follow through strike

After practicing the previous drill, outnumbered combatants should start practicing following through the backward sweep with a second strike, though doing so will require taking another forward step. Doing so allows for outnumbered combats to have more options and, therefore, be less predictable. Nevertheless, it requires being skilled in all the different variants of the sweep from above and the backward sweep that were previously covered, since this strategy forces outnumbered combatants to constantly change the side on they hold their weapon upon squaring off with the opponent approaching from behind.

Performing a follow through strike after the backwards sweep

A)

B)

C)

D)

E)

F)

G)

H)

I)

J)

K)

Combat against three opponents

Overall guideline pertaining positioning

When facing three opponents, and should they be skilled combatants who spread the floor effectively in order to surround their prey, they will form a triangle. In this case, outnumbered combatants should keep themselves on the outside of the triangle, so as to maintain all opponents in their field of view.

Incorrect (A) & correct (B) positioning

A)

B)

Staff

Step one

With three opponents forming a triangle in front the outnumbered combatant, he / she should place him / herself enough on the outside so that, by looking towards the centre, all opponents are kept in the outnumbered combatant's field of view.

Then, outnumbered combatants should simply turn towards their dominant side in order to perform a sweep from above towards the opponent positioned on that same side. Note that when performing such sweep from above against three opponents, and contrary to what was performed against two opponents, the outnumbered combatant should maintain his / her eyesight directed towards the centre of the triangle.

By performing additional identical sequences of sweep from above towards the opponent on the dominant side and the backward sweep towards the opposite opponent, outnumbered combatants are able to apply the same principals previously developed and, therefore, successfully push one opponent away at the same time that they increase the gap towards the remaining opponents.

**Sweep from above towards the opponent
on the dominant side**

A)

B)

C)

D)

Then, while stepping back, the outnumbered combatant should follow this initial technique with a backward sweep towards the opponent approaching from behind.

Backward sweep towards the opponent non dominant side

A)

B)

C)

D)

Step two

The previous drill should now be repeated only, this time around, while having the group of assailants actively seeking to surround the outnumbered combatant.

While performing the backwards sweep, the opponent previously attacked should try to retain striking distance while simultaneously trying to move towards the outnumbered combatant's back

A)

B)

C)

D)

How should outnumbered combatants solve this challenge?

Initially, the first strategy which outnumbered combatants have the tendency of performing consists of slightly adjusting their positioning by stepping sideways and always a bit backwards when performing both the sweep from above and the backward sweep. Doing so enables them to compensate for their opponents' attempts to surround them and, ultimately, keep them in front of them and, hence, clearly within their field of view.

However, this strategy raises one big problem, which is the fact that, if repeated several times, has outnumbered combatants getting cornered after compensating several times for their opponents' surrounding motions. Therefore, a better way of solving this problem consists of using the opponents' surrounding motions against them:

- As the "attackers" try to surround the outnumbered combatant, they increase the distance between themselves. Consequently, by having the opponent on the dominant side step towards the outnumbered combatant's back as he / she performs a backward sweep, this will increase the space between this combatant and the one in the middle.

- Hence, outnumbered combatants should follow through with a sweep from above towards this opponent who is approaching from behind, only by sliding their lead foot before taking a forward step with the back leg. This allows them to push the opponent back and still finish the sweep from above by stepping over the imaginary line that connects that combatant with the one in the middle.

- Finally, by performing a short spin, outnumbered combatants are able to maintain all three opponents in their field of view and, consequently, promptly follow through with a strike towards the opponent who was initially placed in the middle but is now approaching from behind.

By systematically repeating this same strategy, outnumbered combatants will move to a different side of the triangle after each backward sweep. After performing this change of positioning towards the dominant side for three consecutive times, outnumbered combatants will return to the side of the triangle they started from.

As combatant X performs a backward sweep towards O3, O1 approaches while also moving towards X's back, which increases the distance between O1 and O2

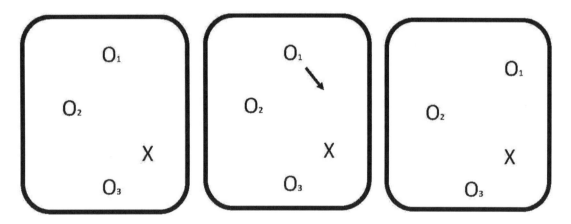

**Performing a sweep from above in order to take advantage
of the opponents' surrounding motion**

A)

B)

C)

D)

E)

F)

G)

Step three

This time around, as the combatant on the dominant side tries to surround the outnumbered combatant while the latter performs the backward sweep, the opponent positioned in the middle realizes that he / she should move towards his / her partner in order to reduce the distance between them, under the overall goal of making it tougher for the outnumbered combatant to change to that side.

Realizing that O1's motion will open the gap between them, O2 opts to move towards O1 so as to close that gap

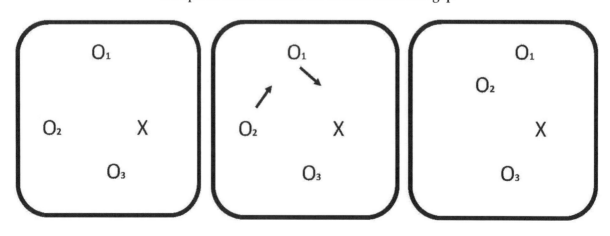

However, though this strategy closes the gap on one side, it increases the gap between the opponent in the middle and his / her other partner. Therefore, when the outnumbered combatant finishes the backward strike towards the opponent on his / her non dominant side under these circumstances, he / she should follow with a sweep from above towards the opponent in the middle position.

Changing sides towards the opponent in the middle
as result of the opponents' different positioning

A)

B)

C)

D)

E)

F)

G)

H)

I)

Similarly to that which was previously performed when changing sides towards the opponent on the dominant side, this sweep from above needs to be initiated by moving the dominant lower limb towards the opponent whom the outnumbered combatant is approaching. Again, doing so allows for the second step performed by the outnumbered combatant to place him / her on the outside of the triangle formed by the opponents.

Additionally, upon finishing the sweep from above which was used to change towards a different side of the triangle, outnumbered combatants should, once again, follow through with a sweep from above towards the opponent who is approaching from behind.

Given that outnumbered combatants should step towards a different side of the triangle after performing each backward sweep, upon changing sides three times by always stepping towards the opponent in the middle, outnumbered combatants will return to the side they started from.

As previously described, the outnumbered combatant should follow the change of side with an immediate sweep from above towards the opponent pushed away before changing sides

A)

B)

C)

D)

Step four

After becoming acquainted with these two tactical options by practicing them separately, trainees should start practicing them within the same drill, which can include the following options:

1) Moving through the triangle made up by the opponents by performing three changes of side clock wise followed by three more changes of side counter clock wise.

2) Afterwards, trainees should start free sparring by having their opponents moving randomly. This will require for outnumbered combatants to finish the backward sweep while already checking out the position of the remaining opponents.

As the outnumbered combatant does so, he / she has to diagnose which side offers more space for him / her to step into. Upon doing so, he / she should perform a sweep from above while taking two steps towards that greater opening.

**Finishing the backward sweep while already
evaluating the remaining combatants' positioning**

A)

B)

C)

D)

**Finishing the backward sweep under different circumstances,
with the biggest opening varying according to the opponents' displacement**

A)

B)

Step five

Last, though certainly not least, trainees should make their free sparring a bit more complex by means of adding the previously analysed skill of engaging multiple opponents.

To do so, and since three opponents will give outnumbered combatants even less space to move between them, performing a first sweep from above in order to immediately change sides is completely out of the question. Instead, outnumbered combatants need to perform the engagement technique already learnt, which has outnumbered combatants starting by taking the initiative towards the opponent on their non dominant side in order to spread the floor a bit better before committing to a change of side.

**Drawing in the opponents and taking the initiative
against the one on the dominant side**

A)

B)

C)

D)

E)

From this position either perform a sweep from above while immediately changing sides straight ahead or towards the opponent on the dominant side, or simply spread the opponents a bit more by performing a sequence of a sweep from above and a backward sweep before eventually gathering the necessary conditions (space) to change sides.

Baton

The use of the baton within this combat scenario will follow the same concepts, with just a few slight adjustments being required.

Step one

After practicing with single handed weapons the training sequence previously described for the staff by performing the sweep from above on the non dominant side, trainees should undergo the exact same sequence for the sweep from above on the dominant side.

Taking the initiative with single handed weapons against the opponent on the dominant side

A)

B)

C)

D)

**Following through by changing sides, while performing
the sweep from above on the dominant side**

A)

B)

C)

D)

E)

Step two

Afterwards, trainees should introduce the following variation which is specific of the baton.

Instead of always performing the full double strike sweep from above, outnumbered combatants should limit its use for when changing sides. After changing sides, outnumbered combatants ought to follow through towards the opponent approaching from behind by merely performing the first strike of the sweep from above. Doing so will solicit taking only a half approaching step in the opponent's direction.

This interruption of the sweep from above serves the purpose of allowing for outnumbered combatants to be quicker in striking the opponent who was initially pushed away while changing sides. This strategy is fundamental in managing aggressive opponents who manage to exert pressure much faster with these shorter weapons.

**Following the change of side with a sequence
of one strike towards each opponent**

A)

B)

C)

D)

E)

F)   ~

G)

H)

I)

After getting a good feel for this strategy, trainees should alternate between following their changes of side with the full double strike sweep from above and only its first strike. Once again, practicing these strategies by alternating between them will make it easier for trainees to retain these similar yet slightly different tactical options.

Step three

Afterwards, trainees need to repeat the previous training sequence for the sweep from above on the dominant side.

Step four

Lastly, trainees should practice performing the full double strike sweep from above mainly when changing sides, while following through the backward sweep with a second strike. Each time that the backward sweep is followed with a second strike outnumbered combatants will, again, be forced to change the side on which they are performing the sweep from above.

SPECIAL NOTES

When facing four opponents, these will constitute the four corners of the four lines which connect them. However, this will change outnumbered combatants' strategy and technique in absolutely nothing since, after each backward sweep, they will simply have to decide on whether to change towards the left or right side.

After pushing away the opponent on the left, the outnumbered combatant (x) has to read whether he / she should step towards the front / left or right.

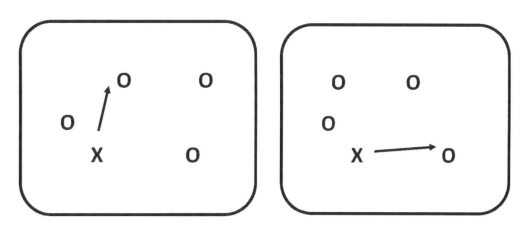

Though outside of the scope of this introductory book, the development of combat skill for outnumbered scenarios also includes the following settings of higher complexity:

- Combat against five or more opponents,

- Two combatants against a higher number of opponents,

- Combat in narrow locations,

- Combat with traditional bladed staffs.

The historical link to single combat

I imagine that some readers might have found it strange that, in the photos presented, the outnumbered combatant was constantly attacking and never forced to parry. To the inexperienced eye it seems that the group of opponents are just passively allowing their opponent to move around, but that is not the case. As I explained during the explanation of the main guidelines for engaging groups of opponents, what is the use of initiating a strike from a distance you have no chances of reaching the opponent with? None whatsoever! Therefore, by standing still and luring in one's opponents, outnumbered combatants can deceive them into assuming false premises and, consequently, take them by surprise with pre-emptively strikes during their approach. Consequently, this means that in "real" combat:

1) The first opponent whom outnumbered combatants attack is, usually, taken by surprise and, quite often, hit.

2) At the same time that outnumbered combatants approach that first opponent, they also distance themselves from the remaining opponents. Therefore, this has these other opponents still finding themselves out of striking distance and sensing the need to approach more so as to position their "prey" within striking distance. Thus, as they do so, outnumbered combatants use this same "trick" and approach yet another of the approaching opponents with yet another pre-emptively strike that forces them into a defensive role.

Given that outnumbered combatants have several different options available to them, they are able to continuously take the initiative and relegate their opponents to defensive reactive roles. Consequently, by stealing the initiative from their opponents and never relinquishing it, outnumbered combatants are continuously able push some opponents away while increasing the distance towards the remaining opponents and, therefore, successfully use the same concept over and over again. Ultimately, this allows for outnumbered combatants to avoid having to even deal with strikes from their opponents, as the latter are always either parrying or out of striking distance, as well as one step behind in this game of juggling distance.

Of course that this all happens in an ideal situation in which outnumbered combatants have good distance management skills while also being capable of swiftly making the transition between moving in different directions as a result of proper body control.

Outside of this ideal world, outnumbered combatants might find themselves finishing one strike against an opponent while having another opponent closer than would be expected and, therefore, able to initiate a strike of his / her own. When this happens, and as explained during the introduction of the sweep from above, outnumbered combatants are to continue their "normal" motion so as to sweep their opponent's strike by means of the first portion of the sweep from above[41]. Given outnumbered combatants' need to square off with opponents positioned in different directions, these half rotational parrying motions end up generating more than enough momentum to sweep through opponents' strikes. Consequently, they are designated as "in motion parries".

**Sweeping an opponent's strike
before following through with a counter attack**

A)

---

[41] Before following through with a counter attack.

B)

C)

D)

E)

This summary of the concepts previously presented is meant support the explanation on the historical and technical evolution of combat skills which I'm about to present.

When people have to deal with either self defence conflicts or battlefields, which type of combat is more common, single combat or outnumbered combat? Undoubtedly the latter.

Therefore, people who live under this type of pressure to perform so as to live another day will, obviously, focus their training on developing the skills required to succeed in this type of environment. Hence, this has combatants focusing on the development of the above mentioned sweeping in motion parries.

Now it is time for a little bit of simple logic and common sense. I have been told that Russians have a saying which goes something like, if you only have a hammer treat everything like a nail. I find this to be very true, given that, at one time or another, we are all confronted with problems that require an ideal set of skills we lack and, whenever this happens, we simply look to do as well as we possibly can by adapting the skills we are in possession off at that moment in time.

A more specific example was that of combatants who focused their training on developing the skills required for outnumbered combat and, by doing so, when occasionally presented with a conflict against a single opponent, were forced to adapt by making the best possible use of the skills they had. To be more concise, when combatants are mostly, if not only, skilled in performing half rotational swinging parrying techniques so as to intercept opponents' strikes when fighting multiple opponents simultaneously, they are forced to come up with different waiting guards that allow them to make use of these parrying techniques upon being confronted by a single opponent. This meant the creation of backward pointing waiting guards where the weapon is placed either over the head or by one's hip.

Backward pointing waiting guard

As illustrated in the following group of photos, from these waiting guards combatants could react against full rotational strikes by sweeping them and following through with counter attacks.

Application of the sweeping in motion parries to single combat

A)

B)

C)

D)

E)

F)

One thing must be noted though. Being the lower limbs a portion of combatants' body which is quite difficult to protect, especially when resorting to this type of side parry sweeping motions, it is fundamental to perform these sequences of in motion parries and follow through counter attacks by stepping out of opponents' reach when parrying. The reason being that, should combatants opt to perform such parries without exiting[42] when facing strikes randomly targeting different heights, they will, quite often, fail to parry and, by not having distance as a backup, get hit on the lower limbs.

Eventually, as a result of the industrial revolution, cities were created where the once pure martial practice for outnumbered scenarios typical of battlefields and group muggings was transformed into a leisure activity that focused exclusively on single combat. With this type of newfound practice being focused on single combat, new techniques and strategies were progressively created that allowed for greater effectiveness in this type of combat, which entailed the replaced of the previously mentioned backward pointing waiting guards by other more fitting options[43].

This, my fellow martial arts' enthusiasts, is how combat skill developed. Social and cultural conditions motivated trainees to adapt their practice so as to focus on the many different success criteria that varied over time. Additionally, as opponents' own abilities

---

[42] Or even stepping in.

[43] This topic is discussed in great detail in my book that focuses on the development of functional parrying skill.

rose and, thus, made certain strategies previously successful obsolete, combatants were forced to devise new strategies and techniques, a process known to most as EVOLUTION!

Ultimately, by having a better understanding of the circumstances which conditioned the development of each set of skills, combatants are able to perform better when sparring given that they are able to interpret and adapt more effectively to opponents showcasing different sets of skills.

Final Notes

Those who know me either from attending my classes, training with me or simply getting together to talk and have some laughs, are well aware of both my passion for martial arts as well as my enthusiasm and eagerness to help others excel.

Having embraced these recent projects under this same motivation and dedication, I hope to have been able to convey in a straight forward and pleasant way these important concepts regarding an area of martial skill rarely approached, and which I also view as fundamental in developing a practical understanding of the historical and sociological constraints surrounding skill development in martial arts.

Obviously that none of this would ever have been possible without the sacrifice and dedication that other instructors had before me, which enabled this art to persevere through time. Personally, I find that it is more than a "mere" living tradition with unbroken lineage, in the sense that it is a treasure we have been blessed with both from a sociological standpoint and a martial skill perspective. It is a chest with many answers for those interested in interpreting and understanding the past, present and future of martial arts' skills. Wouldn't it be funny if, some 500 years after the Portuguese set out to sea in order to give the world to the world, as eloquently described by renown Portuguese poet Luís de Camões, if the birth of a new martial paradigm would develop from this ancient, though almost forgotten, European combat system preserved by this once great nation.

In this sense, I feel that it is important to recall that Portugal had to earn their independence by force, had to conquer new land so as to extend its territory also by force[44], while also resisting their apparently stronger neighbour's attempts to reconquer them[45]. I am not one to say we are the best, since I do not believe that anyone can claim that and, additionally, I also have a deep respect for many others who also achieved plenty of great successes. However, credit should be given where it is due and, in this sense, we deserve a significant amount of credibility regarding our past military exploits and, more specifically, the combat arts on which they were supported.

Luís Franco Preto
August 2011

---

[44] Which even saw them establishing a "Portuguese" city in northern Africa – Ceuta.
[45] The nation nowadays known as Spain.

ABOUT THE AUTHOR

During the 25 years spent practicing several different martial arts and combat sports, Luís Franco Preto opted to elect Jogo do Pau as his main art of practice and research for the past 16 years. Over this period he served as the Portuguese Federation's technical director during a 6 year span.

Having benefited from having an art dully systematized as a result of the lifelong work of previous Masters such as Master Nuno Curvello Russo, he has been able to focus on the enhancement of training methods. This process led him to undergo an undergrad in physical education (Faculdade de Motricidade Humana) and two masters, one in sports' teaching methodologies (Universidade Lusófona de Humanidades e Tecnologias) and a second in coaching sciences (University of British Columbia).

On a professional level, he has coached both team and individual sports, as well as endurance athletes. However, over the years, his focus has been centred around the practical application of sports sciences towards the optimization of performance within martial arts and combat sports.

Staff, baton and longsword COMBAT SERIES

OPTIMING THE TEACHING CURRICULUM OF TECHNIQUE AND TACTICS

(2nd edition)

Available in B&W and Colour

Understanding and developing footwork

(2nd edition)

Development of parrying skill

(2nd edition)

Jogo do Pau: The ancient art & modern science of Portuguese stick fighting (2nd edition)

Physical conditioning: A movement based approach

From other authors

XV Century king D. Duarte's: The art of riding on every saddle

Medieval horsemanship:
Equitation, hunting and knightly combat with lance and sword

Translation by António Franco Preto

Testimonials

While working with us at Blood and Iron Martial Arts, our skills as a club improved dramatically as a result of his tutelage. Not only did our students gain from Luis' skill as a teacher, but our instructor team benefited immeasurably from his insightful coaching. He was an exemplary training partner, and brilliant coach for our head instructor. Luis is a patient tutor with a keen eye for the minutiae and detail of fine body mechanics. During his tenure at Blood and Iron Martial Arts he quickly became a favourite teacher among our students, and became the Head Coach of our fight team.

Lee Smith, Blood & Iron Martial Arts' lead instructor

Luis Preto's mentality in the martial arts is that if a fighting system cannot be adapted to suit the fighter, it is because it is built around the individuality of the creator, which means it will deteriorate over time and is no good for anyone else. Luis studies your potential as a stick fighter and adapts the technical aspects of the system to your fitness capacity, physical and psychological ability and goals. While respecting the fundamental aspects of the system, it just makes it efficient for you.

Pedro Escudeiro, Aikido instructor & chiropractor

Luis delivers content that is both grounded in solid body mechanics and tactically relevant and applicable to all martial artists regardless of discipline. His 'in-context' approach to training martial skills helps students not only learn but easily apply new techniques outside of drills in an efficient and effective manner. He has certainly had a positive impact on the way that I teach and train.

Devon Boorman, Academie Duello's lead instructor

I'm a proud owner of your book of JdP, and am a great fan of both yourself and your work. Your dream of building the art of Jogo do Pau, and all of historical European fighting arts is contagious and irresistible. More, the research you've done, as embodied in your knowledge and obvious skill, not to mention your reputation as one our greatest, while still youngest masters today...well, it's hard to overstate the contribution you're making. Another point I must praise is the modern scientific basis of so much that you write. You have won your spot as one of the leading researcher/practitioners today, who can express both modern sports science and ancient principles together.

Pasquale Scopelliti, HEMA practitioner

I didn't take your JDP class at Fectschule America, but when I saw how you could apply your fencing techniques to longsword (and possibly other styles) I was impressed.

Gray Bennett, HEMA practitioner

Luis Preto teaching is second to none! I`m in the Martial Arts for 12 years already and I can say for my experience that what he is teaching about posture, biomechanics, movement in and footwork in combat scenarios is applied also in other fields of martial arts. He will always be a big influence for me and I will be grateful to him for all my life. Rarely can you see updated scientific approach mixed with original methodologies applied in the field combat. Obrigado Luis!

Pedro Silva, FMA instructor

I had the pleasure of meeting Luis Preto at the 2nd Arts of Mars WWOLC in Germany, mid 2010. With interest I followed his lecture on methodologies in teaching martial arts and a workshop Jogo Do Pau. Not only was I amazed by Luis' footwork and agility, the skills of Jogo Do Pau were certainly of interest to me in relation to practicing longsword. I got to know Luis as a person who takes teaching very serious though who's also very funny, even if you serve him a non-alcoholic drink ;-). Luis' enthusiasm and willingness to share knowledge make him today an important representative of Jogo Do Pau worldwide, and a prominent figure in the world of Historical European Martial Arts.

Alwin Goethals, Swarta's lead instructor (HEMA)

3558936R00100

Made in the USA
San Bernardino, CA
08 August 2013